CONTENTS

GU00888691

Cover illustration: Lord Leverhulme and a plan of the bungalow

A view of Rivington

INTRODUCTION

This booklet gives an account of the life of the first Lord Leverhulme from his childhood in Victorian Bolton to his death in 1925 at the age of seventy-four. During his life Lord Leverhulme was involved in a remarkably varied number of activities, mainly in the North West of England but also throughout the British Isles and the World. These are described in the following chapters.

The town of Bolton and the nearby country area of Rivington were, however, focal points in his life and were especially important to him. The Rivington area is typical of the West Pennine Moors and comprises a pleasant landscape of moorland, farmland, woodland, settlements and reservoirs. The five reservoirs in the area were built in the second half of the nineteenth century to supply the city of Liverpool with water. The village of Rivington with its church, chapel and houses clustered around a small village green, has all the appearances of a traditional English hamlet.

The landscape is dominated by Rivington Pike, 1,184 feet high, surmounted by a squat, square tower, built in 1733 on the site of an ancient fire beacon. The Pike has been popular with visitors for many years and on Sundays and public holidays it is usually crowded with people. Its popularity is such that even in 1835 a local magistrate complained of "the shameful scenes by which the Sabbath is invariably desecrated arising out of the habit of parties going in cartloads on that day to Rivington Pike . . . to indulge in scenes of riot and drunkeness that are a disgrace to a Christian Community". In the same year a special constable was appointed to prevent people going to the Pike on Sundays. Popularity was enhanced by the belief that the atmosphere at the top of the Pike would help cure whooping cough in children, because it was thought to be 'Blackpool air'.

Lord Leverhulme's love of the area may well have stemmed from visits to the Pike when he was a child and his father, James Lever, had attended Rivington School from 1819 to 1823. These attachments to Rivington undoubtedly kindled his desire to improve the area and to make it more accessible to the people of Bolton. This led him, in later years, to establish Lever Park between Rivington and Horwich and to create his now famous gardens on the slopes of the Pike.

The new business premises, Victoria Street, Bolton

William's personal ambition was to be an architect but his father had other plans for him; at fifteen William had to leave school and join the family's wholesale grocery business. One of his first tasks was cutting and wrapping soap which, like most other commodities at that time, arrived in bulk from the manufacturers and had to be cut and wrapped by the grocer. William also learned to discern the quality of products by their taste or smell, an important skill in those days when there were no brand names to differentiate products for consumers. In this, the early stage of his business career, William Lever earned one shilling a week; a sum that would finance perhaps one visit to the theatre or a trip to Manchester.

8

Lever's father promoted him to the accounts section of the firm, and here William introduced a new system of book-keeping. Meanwhile the business was flourishing and James Lever changed his premises from Manor Street to Victoria Street, opposite the newly built Town Hall. In 1870 William Lever became a traveller for the firm. This entailed visiting all the retail grocery shops in Bolton, collecting orders and delivering them on his next round.

In 1872 James Lever made William a partner with a salary of £800 a year. With such a generous income in support of his claims to her affection, William felt bold enough to propose to his childhood sweetheart, Elizabeth Hulme. She accepted, and on the 15th April 1874, they were married at St. George's Road Congregational Church in Bolton.

They spent their honeymoon in Devon and Cornwall and on their return went to live at 2, Park Street, Bolton. Lever soon began planning improvements to their new home and for the rest of his life whenever Lever acquired a new property he would plan alterations to it, so much so that his wife once complained that her house never seemed to be free of workmen. William took great pleasure in employing craftsmen and no expense was spared in allowing their skills free range. He often engaged the services of his architect friend Jonathan Simpson on his building projects as well as being heavily involved himself in the design work.

2, Park Street, Bolton

CHAPTER TWO

The Soap Empire

Lever continued to work as a traveller for the firm; in his zeal for expansion he was soon collecting orders from outside Bolton and found several customers in Wigan. As groceries sold by the Lever Wholesale Grocery Company had to pass through Wigan, on their journey from the port of Liverpool to Bolton, William Lever decided that the firm should establish a branch in Wigan to cut out the unnecessary journey. There already was a wholesale grocery business in Wigan, Ormerod and Co., but as they were in decline Lever bought them out and took over their premises on Wallgate. William Lever became manager of this branch, and he and his wife moved to 21, Upper Dicconson Street in Wigan.

Lever now had the opportunity to put some of his ideas about business practice into operation. He sent agents to Ireland to improve the system of importing fresh butter and eggs; he bought direct from manufacturers whenever possible to cut out the middleman, and made increasing use of advertising to promote goods sold by Lever and Company. These methods were very successful and helped to establish the firm as the largest wholesale grocery business between Liverpool and Manchester. In 1881 the Levers moved back to Bolton and into 'Westcombe', a large house on Victoria Road.

In 1884, at the age of 33, William Lever was considering retirement; he thought of buying one of the Orkney Islands and living out his life peacefully there. However, he abandoned this idea and decided to market a product of his own brand with a distinctive trademark that no-one else could copy. Lever chose the name 'Sunlight' and used it on a variety of soaps produced by several different manufacturers. The soap, in ready-cut tablets packed in cartons, was launched onto the market accompanied by an extensive advertising campaign.

Sunlight gets the Washing done Leaving Time for Sport and Fun.

Lever aimed his advertising at working people, hoping to convince them that soap was no longer a luxury but an essential household item. One advertisement, entitled "Why does a woman look old sooner than a man?" put forward the argument that not only did Sunlight soap wash clothes cleaner than other soaps, but was also better for the complexion than its rivals. According to one poem Sunlight even halted the ageing process:

"T'will make your brow a snowy white,
As free from grief and care,
As when with youth your eyes were bright,
And cheeks beyond compare . . .
This article, if you but try,
Will realise each hope,
Go send your maid at once, and buy
A box of Sunlight Soap".

The factory at Warrington

This type of advertising was very successful and sales of the soap rose dramatically. However, the soap manufacturers began charging Lever higher and higher prices for their products and he soon reached the decision that he must manufacture his own soap.

In 1885 Lever persuaded his reluctant father, who believed that a 'cobbler should stick to his last', to lend him money to buy a factory at Warrington. William's brother James agreed to join him in the venture. The brothers were fortunate at Warrington in retaining the services of Percy J. Winser as works manager and Edward Wainwright who was a highly skilled soap boiler. The soap they developed was more effective than other brands because it was made from vegetable oil instead of tallow, allowing it to lather more freely.

Sales of the soap continued to rise and soon the Sunlight trademark was known all over Britain. Lever made various alterations to the Warrington factory to expand its capacity and by 1887 it was producing 450 tons of soap a week. This was still not enough to meet the ever increasing demand but a disagreement with the landlord over ground rent meant that he was unable to expand the factory. Lever began looking out for a freehold site with good road and water communications where he could build his own factory. In 1887, Lever's architect, William Owen, selected a site near Birkenhead and Lever purchased it, ensuring that he had plenty of land on which to expand. Construction of the factory began in 1888 and by January 1889 soap production was underway. That same year work began on the industrial village intended for the workforce.

The cottages at Port Sunlight

The village of Port Sunlight was a typical example of nineteenth century industrial philanthropy, a philosophy subscribed to not only by Lever but by other major manufacturers of the time. It centred on the belief that if employees were healthy they would, in consequence, work harder, and be more loyal to the company. Lever believed that capital and labour shared a unity of interests; his recipe for a successful business was, "the production of more goods with less labour in fewer hours, so as to allow for larger wages and a bigger margin for profit". The industrial village of Bournville near Birmingham built by Cadbury Brothers was a similar exercise in industrial philanthropy.

Lever, perhaps remembering the confined and claustrophobic rows of terraced houses from the Bolton of his childhood, ensured that the layout of the village incorporated as many open spaces as possible. The houses, in a variety of architectural styles, were built in small groups, all with front and back gardens. Each house had a kitchen, scullery, parlour and either three or four bedrooms. Port Sunlight village also had public buildings; two large schools, a museum, library and cottage hospital. The village pub was originally unlicensed, in accordance with Lever's views on temperance. However, when the villagers were consulted on the matter they voted overwhelmingly in favour of lifting the ban on alcohol, so Lever gave way to popular feeling.

Pegging out a Claim for
SUNLIGHT

No extravagant claims are made for

Sunlight Soap.
IT IS PURE.

The white, sweet, linen on the line

proclaims this.

As proof, £1,000 is offered for any adulteration
found in its composition.

LEVER BROTHERS, LIMITED, PORT SUNLIGHT, ENGLAND.
THE NAME LEVER ON SOAP IS A GUARANTEE OF PURITY AND EXCELLENCE.

By 1914 the village was complete. As its population was restricted to Lever Brothers employees, anyone who was dismissed from the firm lost their home as well as their job. Lever had created some of the best working class housing in the country, which must have gone some way towards ensuring a compliant workforce.

Attempts were made by Lever to ensure a high moral tone in the village and he barred some of his employees from living there, because he felt they had 'objectionable habits'. In the winter the Company arranged dances. Girls under eighteen had their partners provided for them by the firm, and those above that age had to submit the names of their partner to the works social department for approval.

Lever expected all those in his employ to work extremely hard. At the Port Sunlight factory he had a glass office built for himself above the clerks' working area to see at a glance if any were slacking. He could then administer a reprimand via the nearest works manager. Lever once employed a private detective to follow the daily movements of an employee at the New York branch of the Company, because he had heard reports of the fellow's laziness. Perhaps it is not too surprising that, despite its attractions, some Lever Brothers employees turned down the chance to live at Port Sunlight.

A view of Port Sunlight

Lord Leverhulme and Family

In 1888 the Levers' only child, William Hulme Lever was born, and six months later the family left Bolton and moved to Thornton Manor, near the village of Thornton Hough on the Wirral Peninsula.

The move enabled Lever to be near Port Sunlight and to use the house as a place for consultation with managers, as well as allowing parties from his workforce to picnic in the Manor grounds. Thornton Manor became one of the most important of the family homes and Lever made many alterations and additions to it. He also took a benevolent interest in the nearby village of Thornton Hough, initiating several building schemes whereby old houses were knocked down and replaced by new ones with modern amenities.

CHAPTER THREE

Public and Private Life

The move to Thornton Manor ushered in perhaps the busiest and most public phase of Lever's life. It was from this time that he became a serious art collector with the continuing success of the business enabling him to fully indulge in his eclectic taste. Any spare rooms at Thornton Manor needed to be used and as with all the houses that Lever acquired he filled them full with works of art. His collection became extensive, including eighteenth, nineteenth and early twentieth century British paintings and sculptures, Chinese porcelain of the sixteenth and nineteenth centuries, English china, pottery and Wedgewood. In addition he built up smaller collections of silver pewter, Egyptian antiquities and folk-life material.

Lever also became deeply involved in politics. He gave lectures on various issues all over the North-West. One of his favourite topics was the case for a six-hour day. He supported this measure because he felt both industrialist and worker would benefit; the employee would work-harder, produce more goods and have time available for 'uplifting' activities. This is a typical example of the enlightened self-interest which characterised many of Lever's actions as an employer.

Thornton Manor

Lever by Sir Luke Fildes

In July 1892 he stood as the Liberal candidate for Birkenhead in the Parliamentary Elections. This was a seat unlikely to be won by the Liberal party at that time. Although he lost the election, Lever did however manage to increase the Liberal vote in the area.

He actually seemed to prefer losing seats because it gave him the opportunity to state his beliefs without being restricted to wearisome Parliamentary life. When in 1906 Lever was elected Member of Parliament for Wirral in the Liberal landslide victory of that year, his victory election must have been tinged somewhat with regret; he had after all, little time in his busy life to play the part of a conscientious Member of the Commons. However, for four years Lever dutifully attended Parliament and championed many Liberal causes, as well as putting forward a scheme of alterations to the House of Commons. After 1910 he happily returned to contesting seats he had very little chance of winning.

Over the years Lever developed quite a spartan lifestyle; he started his day at 4.30am with a few exercises and a cold bath. Whenever possible he slept in an open air bedroom with only a glass canopy sheltering his head. All his houses had one of these bedrooms constructed on the roof. For the rest of the day until 5.30pm Lever would work, sparing only fifteen minutes for a light lunch. In his physical appearance he was described by one reporter as a 'typical John Bull'; five feet five inches tall with a tendency towards stockiness. His dress was always simple and usually in the same style. Lever and his wife travelled extensively, visiting various obscure parts of the globe and making three around-the-world trips. These trips, rarely undertaken for pleasure alone, were usually the means by which Lever supervised the expansion of his Company into countries all over the world.

It was on his frequent visits to America that Lever picked up most of his advertising techniques, some of which were regarded as highly controversial. He initiated the prize system in Britain whereby a stated number of Sunlight Soap wrappers earned the collector an extravagant gift. At one time 250,000 soap wrappers won a £250 motorcar. Other manufacturers were forced into copying Lever's methods but eventually the system became self-defeating as sales always dropped dramatically if a prize was not offered. Lever and the other soap manufacturers had to enter into a common agreement to discontinue the system.

Another souce of controversy was Lever's use of works of art in his advertisements. In 1899 he bought a picture called 'The New Frock' by the artist Frith. It was of a little girl holding up a white pinafore. The picture later appeared in Sunlight Soap advertisements with the words, "So Clean" added, somewhat to the chagrin of the artist and provoking quite a debate in the national newspapers of the day.

Lever also distributed copies of his Sunlight Year Book free to elementary schools, a publicity stunt other soap companies regarded as impertinent.

In 1894 the business became Lever Brothers Limited, a public company, which by the end of the century was one of the largest soap companies in the world, with factories in Europe, South Africa and Canada. Their products went on to include Lifebuoy, Lux, Vim and Monkey-Brand as Lever bought out other companies.

In the early years of the twentieth century, palm and coconut oils, the raw materials needed for soap making, began to rise in price causing a ripple of anxiety to pass through the soap industry. Lever averted any possible difficulties by buying up large areas of land in regions where palm trees flourished. In 1906 he acquired land in the Solomon Islands in the Pacific, in 1910 he bought six million acres in the Belgian Congo and in 1911 he acquired property in Nigeria. Lever even bought a fleet of ships to transport the palm oil straight to his factories and therefore ensured that the company controlled the

manufacturing process from start to finish.

In 1904 Lever bought another house, this time in London on the edge of Hampstead Heath. True to form he made many alterations to 'The Hill' as the house was called. The garden was landscaped and a pergola built around the grounds to ensure privacy. Local residents and users of the Heath felt that the alterations spoiled the landscape and reacted with hostility to any attempts on Lever's part to extend his grounds.

CHAPTER FOUR

Lever the Benefactor

Lever did not just spend money on improving his own surroundings. He was also prepared to use the vast profits he made from his soap business to finance schemes he felt would be of more general benefit. He believed that it was his duty to repay, "the debt which every man owes to his native town". Consequently he spent a lot of money on schemes relating to Bolton. In 1895 he and his brother James built a new Congregational Church on Blackburn Road, in memory of their father. Lever also built three other churches: Christ Church at Port Sunlight in 1902, St. George's Church at Thornton Hough in 1905 and Neston Congregational Church, near Thornton Hough, in 1906.

In 1898 Lever bought Hall i'th Wood in Bolton, the house where Samuel Crompton built the first spinning mule. Lever had the building carefully restored and presented it as a gift to Bolton in 1902. He bought many items of period furniture and developed the house into one of the first folk-life museums in the country. He established several other museums and art galleries, the Lever Free Library and Museum at Port Sunlight in 1903. Rivington Hall in 1911 and Hulme Hall and the Lady Lever Art Gallery at Port Sunlight which opened in 1922. Lever believed that art should be accessible to everyone, as it was a means of education and would bring about moral improvement.

Hall i' th' Wood

Lever became a governor of Bolton School in 1898, which at that time occupied only a small building near the Parish Church. In 1899 he bought a house on Chorley New Road for the school to move into. He maintained strong links with the School over the years and in 1913 established the New Lever Trust to amalgamate the Grammar School with the Girls' High School to form Bolton School. Lever planned to construct a magnificent building on Chorley New Road and he selected the final design from the entries of several architects. Unfortunately, Lever never saw the building completed as work on it only began in 1925, the year of his death.

The Leverhulme family have continued to take a strong interest in the School and the present Lord Leverhulme is head of the Board of Governors. Bolton School was not the only educational establishment to benefit from Lever's generosity, in 1907 he provided the means for the University of Liverpool to establish schools in Town Planning, Tropical Medicine and Russian Studies, subjects in which Lever himself took a keen interest. In 1919 he endowed the Chair of Physical Chemistry at the University of Bristol and in 1923 he contributed to a new science building at the University of Edinburgh.

Bolton School

William Lever had lavish schemes for the redevelopment of Bolton. He employed the architect Thomas H. Mawson to draft out these ideas, and the results were published in 'Bolton - A Study in Civic Art and Town Planning', which appeared in 1911. The same ideas were also depicted in 'Bolton - as it is and as it might be', published in 1916. Lever's vision was of wide boulevards linking the main features of the town, with a series of connecting parks on its perimeter. He took a step towards this by buying 98 acres of land on the east side of the town, now Leverhulme Park, and donating it to Bolton in 1918 during his term as Mayor. The town council sadly never adopted his scheme, even though he offered to pay something towards the cost.

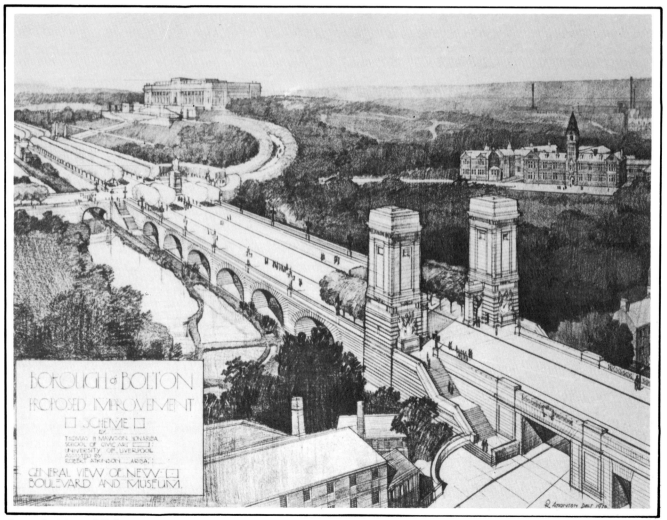

Levers' vision of Bolton

CHAPTER FIVE

Lever Park

Undoubtedly Lever's most generous gift to Bolton was the area of countryside between Rivington and Horwich known as Lever Park. In 1899 the owner of the Rivington Hall Estate, Mr. J.W. Crompton, asked Lever if he would be interested in buying the area. The estate comprised 2,110 acres of moorland surrounding the Pike, part of which acted as gathering grounds for the reservoirs supplying the city of Liverpool with water. Lever was definitely interested in purchasing the area; he saw it as an ideal gift for the people of Bolton which would also provide him with an opportunity to indulge his passion for landscape design. However, he insisted that Liverpool Corporation be given the chance to buy the area if they wished in order to safeguard the purity of their water supply. Liverpool was offered the estate at the price Lever was willing to pay, £60,000, but they turned it down and so the transaction was made between Lever and Crompton.

Work began on providing amenities for visitors to the Park almost as soon as Lever assumed ownership, but in the spring of 1902 his plans received a setback. Liverpool Corporation, alarmed at all the building activity in the vicinity of their reservoirs, promoted a Bill through Parliament to obtain statutory powers over the land feeding the reservoirs. This included Lever's house and 45 acres of ground, which he had retained for his personal use when he donated the remainder of the estate to Bolton Corporation in 1902 for use as a public park. Not surprisingly Lever objected strongly to this move and with the legal help of H.M. Asquith and F.E. Smith he fought the legislation in court. The case had to be settled before a Select Committee of the House of Commons; the final decision reached in 1905 ruled that Lever was to keep his house and grounds, while the park had to be bought by Liverpool at almost twice the price Lever had paid for it. Not only that, but Liverpool Corporation had to maintain the area as a park and continue to let the public have free access to its amenities. When the Corporation appealed against this decision, not only did the Committee reinforce its provisions but it also declared that the area should be called 'Lever Park'.

Rivington Hall

A replica of the ruins of Liverpool Castle

Lever had carried on with his building projects throughout the duration of the case, perhaps a sign of his optimism about the outcome. He built a number of roads connecting Bolton, Rivington and Belmont. Within the area of the Park itself he built long straight roads which converge on a replica of the ruin of Liverpool Castle. Trees were then planted on both sides of the roads successfully establishing typical examples of the vista effect Lever was trying to create. The ruin, built on a rise of land next to the Lower Rivington Reservoir, was begun in 1912. Unfortunately, Lever never witnessed the completion of the castle; construction dragged on after his death since only a few workmen were employed on it at any one time.

Other projects were executed more swiftly: the two barns, of possible Saxon origin, were renovated to serve as refreshment rooms for the many visitors to the Park. Lever built on new walls and side-aisles, but the original roof supports can still be seen inside. He also converted Rivington Hall into a museum and displayed many items there from his own art collection. The Hall was opened to the public in 1911. Several of the nearby fields were enclosed to form paddocks in which he placed exotic animals and birds. In 1915, a Bolton man living in Australia even sent a gift of four kangaroos to add to the collection.

The ceremony opening the Park took place on the 18th May 1904 at Rivington Hall Barn, even though the legal battle with Liverpool was not yet over. Five hundred guests were present and Lever invited his old schoolmaster, W.T. Mason, to formally open the Park. Each guest was given a presentation copy of a book on the history of Rivington, written by W. Fergusson Irvine and commissioned by Lever. By 1911 most of Lever's plans for the Park had been realised, so another ceremony was held to mark this achievement. Lever had intended to extend the main road through the park southwards into Horwich but this was not undertaken until after his death. His son bore the full cost of this work, and paid for the erection of two obelisks at the entrance to the Park as a memorial to his father.

In 1901 a timber bungalow designed by J. Simpson was built on the moorland slopes beneath the Pike. It was called 'Roynton Cottage' after an old name for Rivington, but was more popularly known simply as 'The Bungalow'. The first bungalow, built of timber, was intended as a temporary residence for shooting weekends and short visits. In 1905 Lever added a second storey supported by steel pillars. He could not have foreseen just how temporary the bungalow was to prove; on the 7th July 1913 it was burned down by a suffragette while the Levers dined elsewhere with the King and Queen. The culprit was Edith Rigby, a very militant member of the suffragette movement. She thought the bungalow was a suitable target because the grandeur of the house and gardens epitomised to Edith Rigby all the inequalities of capitalism. She knew that Lever had connections with the Prince of Wales and Lloyd George, and therefore considered him a legitimate target. Burning down property was a recognised tactic of the suffragettes, who felt that the peaceful campaign of the previous forty years had achieved little; more drastic measures were needed to bring their cause to the attention of the public and the Government.

Roynton Cottage

That night the Rigby's chauffeur, Charles, drove Edith and a friend, Albert Yeadon, to Rivington. Unbeknown to Charles, he was also conveying a large keg full of paraffin which had been stored in Albert's wardrobe waiting to be used at the right moment. The two conspiritors gave Charles a shilling to spend in the 'Black Lad' pub, while they carried the keg up the hillside. Edith then ordered Albert Yeadon to leave, not wanting anyone else to take the blame for her actions. After making sure the bungalow was empty she set fire to it. The resulting conflagration created quite a spectacle for local people. Edith later gave herself up to the police and was imprisoned.

Within a year a new bungalow was built on the same site, this time from local stone and with a flat concrete roof; it was obviously intended to be permanent. The new bungalow cost £30,000 to build and Lever filled it with antiques, tapestries and valuable works of art. Sir Alfred East, the painter and close personal friend of Lever was a frequent guest at the bungalow. During these visits he painted several views of the Rivington landscape which Lever bought and later donated to Bolton Art Gallery in 1911.

The burnt bungalow

The Ballroom

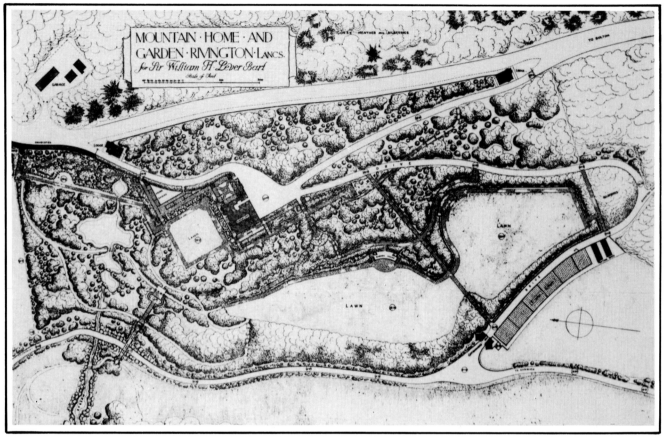

Lever was fond of entertaining on a lavish scale, sometimes having as many as fifty guests at Christmas. On occasions he would throw the whole place open in aid of charitable causes. In his later years Lever became fond of dancing, and in 1920 had a circular ballroom with a minstrels gallery added to the bungalow. The design on the ceiling depicted the arrangement of the constellations on the 18th September 1851, the eve of Lever's birth.

The most impressive of Lever's building projects at Rivington must have been the gardens he created out of the open moorland surrounding his bungalow. Work began on these in 1905 and was to continue until Lever's death in 1925. Once again the architect was Thomas Mawson, but the design was obviously dictated by Lever's tastes and preferences. Local stone and a rugged building style were both employed in an attempt to make the garden appear to be a natural part of the landscape. Archways, flights of steps and crazy paved footpaths linked together the different levels of the gardens and led the walker to the various summerhouses that provided shelter from the moorland climate. A portion of garden called the Garth was constructed like a cloister, specifically to provide shelter on blustery days.

Small pigeon towers and dovecotes were scattered throughout the grounds and these became home for the many doves and pigeons he introduced in the garden. However, the scene is dominated by one pigeon tower in particular, a tall and sometimes eerie-looking edifice standing at the north-eastern corner of the grounds. Built in 1910, it consists of four rooms, one on top of another, connected by a spiral staircase. The architect was Mr. R. Atkinson who also designed some of the nearby loggias and summerhouses.

Rockwork and Waterfall at Roynton Cottage

The Pigeon Tower

The other main features of the grounds were a spacious lawn, laid out in 1906, tennis courts and the 'Japanese Garden' built in 1922. The 'Garden' was probably inspired by Lever's visit to Japan in 1913 and consisted of an artificial lake surrounded by teahouses, lanterns and other Japanese ornaments. The lake fed a series of waterfalls that descended through the woods below the 'Garden'. The upper and lower parts of the grounds were connected by a stone bridge, built in 1910 and reputedly designed by Lever himself.

Planting the garden presented something of a problem because many believed that the moorland would support only its native heather and bilberry. But the pessimists were proved wrong when 150,000 shrubs and trees flourished in the Rivington climate. Lever was very proud of the garden he had created out of barren moorland and loved to take guests on guided walks, pointing out some of its more ingenious contrivances. Lever often had large garden parties and sometimes held the Liberal Party rally there. Every year the girls of Bolton School were invited to an open day in the grounds.

After Lever's death in 1925 the bungalow and grounds were bought by John Magee of Magee Marshall, the local brewers. Magee died in 1939 and the property passed into the hands of Liverpool Corporation. Over the years the bungalow fell into disrepair, and despite attempts to come up with an alternative use for the building nothing could be found and in 1947 it had to be demolished. The gardens were left to deteriorate until all that remained of the once grand home on the moors were ruins overgrown with rhododendron bushes. However, since 1974 the British Trust for Conservation Volunteers, sponsored by the North West Water Authority, have cleared areas of overgrown vegetation and restored some of the features of the gardens.

Levers Bridge or 'Seven Arch' Bridge

The boating lake

The 'Japanese Garden'

CHAPTER SIX

Leverhulme's Later Years

Despite the world wide success of his soap business, Lever's later years were tinged with sorrow and loneliness. His brother, James Darcy Lever, who had worked with him to create Lever Brothers, had a nervous breakdown in 1895 and was forced to retire from business life. His death in 1910 was a severe blow for Lever who had, throughout his life, allowed few people to become close to him. Lever would have missed his brother's support within the Company; he was seldom willing to share his responsibilities with others and liked to be the pivot around which his business revolved. Advice or criticism from subordinates was rarely welcome and all decisions had to be referred to Lever. As the Company continued to expand Lever must have found his omnipotent role within it more and more difficult to maintain without the support of his brother and in later years, without that of his wife.

Lever was created a baronet in 1911 and so became Sir William Lever. In 1912 he and his wife embarked on an expedition to the South Seas and the Belgian Congo to inspect the Company's property there. On returning to England in 1913 Lever immediately began drawing up plans of villages to be built in the areas he had just visited.

In July 1913 he was travelling again, this time to inspect factories on the European continent. He was in Marseilles when he heard that Lady Lever, who had remained in England, was gravely ill with pneumonia. Lever rushed back to England and was with her when she died on the 24th July. She was to be sorely missed by Lever, creating a void which moved him to say, "I am convinced that without her great influence there would have been neither a Port Sunlight, nor a Lever Brothers as we know it today. It came because of the confidence she inspired in me".

Lever departed on a world tour with his son and daughter-in-law in an attempt to shake off his feelings of melancholy and loneliness. The deterioration of his hearing further exacerbated his sense of isolation.

Lever Brothers, with their control over raw material supplies, continued to prosper, especially during the First World War from 1914 to 1918. Glycerine, a by-product of soap manufacture, was needed for making explosives. To replace the rapidly depleting stocks of butter, the Government asked the Company to manufacture margarine which required similar raw materials to soap. The high demand for palm oil certainly paid off Lever's investment in Africa. After the war, Lever continued to expand his sphere of operations in order to gain greater access to the oils essential in soap making. He became involved in the whaling industry and also bought the Niger Company in West Africa.

In June 1917 Lever was raised to the Peerage, adopting the title Lord Leverhulme of Bolton-le-Moors, which compounded his own name with his wife's maiden name. In the same year he bought some land in the Western Isles of Scotland. The island he bought is usually referred to separately as Lewis and Harris because the two areas are joined only by a narrow strip of land. The majority of people who lived there eked out a precarious existence on the few acres of land they occupied known as Crofts. The rough climate and poor quality of the land yielded little for the farmer, which convinced Leverhulme that the only potential for the future lay in the development of the island's fishing industry.

With this aim, Leverhulme established the firm of Macfisheries to handle the sale and distribution of kippers and herrings. He also built a canning factory and an ice-plant at Stornaway, the main town on Lewis, and began building houses and a new road. The people of Lewis, however, did not want to give up their crofts and an independent lifestyle to work for someone else. The most important thing to them was owning their land, not a weekly wage from factory work.

Leverhulme, disappointed in the islanders' attitudes, had to concede defeat and in 1923 abandoned his plans for Lewis and made a gift of the island to its people. He then concentrated all his energies on Harris, where he built several roads, a village called Leverburgh, and a new harbour. However, progress on these schemes was disrupted when Leverhulme was forced to focus all his attentions on his business interests following industrial difficulties within Lever Brothers. It also meant that he had fewer reserves of cash to spend on developing the island. After Leverhulme's death the Company called a halt to all work on Harris.

During this period Leverhulme received many honours. Between 1917 and 1918 he held the office of High Sheriff of Lancashire by appointment of the King and in 1918 he was chosen as Mayor of Bolton. He, therefore, had the pleasant task of organising many of the celebrations in the town to mark the end of the 1914-18 war. Leverhulme also presided over the restructuring of the local rating system and gave his support to many local charities. In 1918, a collection of Leverhulme's many speeches and articles was published, edited by Stanley Unwin. In 1922, Leverhulme was created a Viscount, taking the title Viscount Leverhulme of the Western Isles.

Lord Leverhulme as Mayor

Lord Leverhulme lying-in state

In May 1925 Leverhulme was travelling from the Bungalow at Rivington to his house in Hampstead when he caught a chill, which subsequently developed into pneumonia. He died on the 7th May, aged seventy-four, and was buried next to his wife at Port Sunlight. For his funeral on the 11th May, all work was halted at the factory. A queue of people waiting to pay their last respects stretched for two miles outside the Lady Lever Art Gallery where his body lay in state.

The business empire he created continues today under the name of Unilever, a company formed in 1930 from the merger of Lever Brothers with the Netherlands Company 'Margarine Union'. It continues to thrive and its range of business concerns is vast. One of the largest shareholders in Unilever is the Leverhulme Trust, which finances various beneficient research projects. This Trust was created by Lord Leverhulme in his will, the last philanthropic act of a life which was characterised by benevolence.

Although his philanthropy was at times paternalistic Leverhulme was motivated by a genuine desire to improve the quality of people's lives. Leverhulme once said that the reason why he built the model village of Port Sunlight was so that his workforce would, "know more about the science of life than they can in a back street slum, and in which they will learn that there is more enjoyment in life than in the mere going to and returning from work and looking forward to Saturday night to draw their wages".

At Port Sunlight instead of profit sharing, Leverhulme had what he termed 'prosperity sharing', whereby profits were spent on improving the village for the benefit of the workers. At times Leverhulme appeared to believe that he knew what would be good for other people better than they knew themselves, which partly explains why he achieved so little in Lewis and Harris. Nevertheless, his boundless generosity cannot be denied, and attempts to analyse his benevolence should not diminish its practical value. Many people derive pleasure from visiting Lever Park and exploring the remains of the garden on the moor. Hopefully they will continue to do so for many years to come.

Lord Leverhulme

How do you propose
to do your washing
this leap year ?

Every wash-day brings a proposition.
How is the work to be done to the best
advantage?

USE

Sunlight Soap.

'Twill be for better,
Not for worse.

£1,000 STAKED ON THE PURITY OF EVERY BAR.

LEVER BROTHERS, LIMITED, PORT SUNLIGHT, ENGLAND.

THE NAME LEVER ON SOAP IS A GUARANTEE OF PURITY AND EXCELLENCE.

SUNLIGHT SOAP

*When we are married
we'll use it too*

THE MORAL.

Whilst you can't put OLD HEADS
on YOUNG SHOULDERS you can train
up a child in the way it should go.

LEVER BROTHERS, LIMITED, PORT SUNLIGHT, ENGLAND.

THE NAME LEVER ON SOAP IS A GUARANTEE OF PURITY AND EXCELLENCE.

Sources of Information

Jolly, W.P., "Lord Leverhulme" Constable 1976;
Leverhulme, W.H., Second Viscount Leverhulme,
"William Hesketh Lever, First Viscount Leverhulme"
Unwin Brothers 1927;
Mawson, T.H., "Civic Art Studies in Town Planning,
Parks, Boulevards and Open Spaces" Batsford 1926;
Mawson, T.H., and Mawson, E.P., " The Art and Craft of
Garden Making" Batsford 1926;
Nicolson, N., "Lord of the Isles" Weidenfield and
Nicolson 1960;
Wilson, C., "The History of Unilever" Volumes I, II,
(1954) & Volume III (1968).

Acknowledgements

Photographs by kind permission of Bolton Museum
and Art Gallery, Batsford Publishers Ltd., and St. Regis
Newspapers Ltd. Plans reproduced by kind permission
of Bolton archives.

Published by United Utilities plc. on behalf of the
West Pennine Moors Area Management Committee.

United Utilities plc.
Dawson House, Great Sankey
Warrington. WA5 3LW

www.unitedutilities.com

Printed by N.B. Colour Print Limited, Fellery Street,
Chorley, Lancs. England PR7 1EH

ISBN O 902228 53 6